Table of Contents

Introduction

Welcome to the world of nonviolent action. This manual is less a detailed "how to" and more a big picture approach to direct action. It breaks down some of the myths of nonviolent action and explains the value, power, and rationale for direct action.

This manual was originally written for Casino-Free Philadelphia. At the time, we were preparing for the possibility of a prolonged direct action stand-off. This handbook was written to prepare us and discuss some of the reasons people use direct action.

Its title is a play on a myth spurred by reporters. In April 2007, the Philadelphia Inquirer reported that "Opponents will continue their efforts to block casino development in Philadelphia - even it means lying in front of bulldozers in the future" (*Casino opponents to continue protests no matter*, April 2007).

Through our efforts, we did not end up laying in front of bulldozers. And there are two good reasons. The first is that the process and the sites were so bad that more and more people switched to our position, including politicians (you can read the compelling campaign at www.StrategyAndSoul.org). The second is that you don't *lay* in front of a bulldozer. That's nonsense. If you lay down the bulldozer cannot see you and you have terrible visibility.

However, you might *stand* in front of bulldozers. Though once unauthorized people enter an active construction site, workers are required by law to stop using dangerous equipment and – therefore – the bulldozers will not be moving. So we can end the myth right now that people will be laying in front of bulldozers.

This manual addresses other myths, too. It explains that direct action is not just for rebels, young people, or as an expression of anger – it's something regular citizens do. Nor is direct action contrary to the rule of law that we hold in America – rather, direct action is foundational to maintaining integrity in a democracy.

This manual also takes a glimpse into the moral and legal questions around direct action. It puts a special focus on a set of tactics called *blockades* – used especially to halt destructive development using one's own body.

Because this is a manual – as opposed to a book – it is not designed to simply be read through from cover to cover. It is a resource material, to give access to some key documents. It's especially to be used alongside direct action trainings that Casino-Free Philadelphia offers. Already over three-hundred people have gone through trainings offered by Casino-Free Philadelphia and over fifty have engaged in direct action activities. If necessary, we will continue, by even standing – but not *laying* – in front of bulldozers.

Thanks for your interest in this book!

Warmly,

- Daniel Hunter

What You Need to Know to Use Nonviolent Direct Action

Nonviolent direct action is known by many names. Gandhi called it *satyagraha* (truth or soul force). Henry Thoreau called it *civil disobedience*. Activists in North Philadelphia sometimes call it *street heat*. In the Philippines, democracy activists call it *people power*.

Underneath all of these definitions are similar themes such as a use of tactics outside of normal institutions (use of the street or fasting) and a commitment to refraining from violence. But even more core to all of these is that direct action is about *power* – bringing together people to make a united change.

A Definition of Nonviolent Action

We use a simple definition of nonviolent action:

> *Nonviolent action are techniques outside of institutionalized behavior for waging conflict using methods of protest, noncooperation, and intervention without the use or threat of injurious force.*

In essence, people turn to nonviolent direct action after the institutionalized ways of settling disagreements are unsuccessful. In the civil rights movement, black people turned to nonviolent action after years of fighting in the courts to end institutionalized segregation. The courts did not provide the relief needed, and so nonviolent action was born. The methods of nonviolent action lie outside institutionalized behavior.

In using these methods people either do what they're not expected to do or even forbidden to do, like demand coffee at a segregated lunch counter if they're African American. Or nonviolent action can be refusing to do what they are expected to do (or required to do), like pay a special tax to the English king for the tea they drink.

You with Burmese monks in 2007 protesting the oppressive military junta.

In the casino struggle, nonviolent action was turned to after it became obvious the PGCB and then-elected officials had no interest in protecting the rights of residents and city taxpayers regarding the ills of casinos. The actions included *noncooperation* – such as refusing to cooperate with the PGCB's demands that the public not speak at "public" meetings. Other tactics were doing what we were not expected to do – such as the Citizens' Document Search to get public documents made secret by the PGCB. All of those tactics put pressure on institutions, like the PGCB, but were actions which, of themselves, were outside tradition.

Nonviolent action, therefore, can be distinguished from other forms of doing conflict which are *within* current institutions and traditions, like going to court or competing in an election. They are *not* considered nonviolent action. It was not nonviolent action when Casino-Free Philadelphia (CFP) collected 27,000 signatures to give citizens a vote on the question of if casinos should be built within 1,500-feet of homes, places of worship, and schools. Getting petitions for placing a referendum on the ballot is within the City's rules and therefore institutionalized. But when the Supreme Court stripped the question from the ballot and CFP ran Philly's Ballot Box – running our own election – it was nonviolent direct action.

When the courts, elected officials, and official institutions (like the City Planning Commission) abandon their roles to protect citizens and instead act corruptly, where to turn? People turn to nonviolent direct action after the institutional modes fail.

So why does nonviolent action work? Aren't institutions like the Supreme Court imbued with more power than frustrated citizens? The answer, surprisingly, is no – not when people use their power.

It's All About Power

Traditionally politics is seen as flowing from the top downwards. Those on top have power. A janitor takes orders from their supervisor who takes orders from the district head and so on – all the way up to the President of the United States.

Most institutions in our society are viewed this way: corporations have at their top the CEO, cities have Mayors at the top, and our legal system has a federal Supreme Court. In that view of society everyone below has to follow orders or face consequences: such as being fired, facing political retribution, or being placed in jail.

But that is not the only type of power.

Power also flows up. The CEO is helpless if employees refuse to take their orders. The Mayor is helpless if the citizens withhold their financial support for his initiatives (e.g. refuse to pay taxes), undermine his policies, and collectively refuse to go along with her orders. The Supreme Court is disabled if cities refuse to implement their interpretation of laws.

Direct action uses this form of power: power flowing *from* the bottom upwards. *People power.*

A group in Serbia fighting against a dictator wrote:

> *By themselves, rulers cannot collect taxes, enforce repressive laws and regulations, keep trains running on time, prepare national budgets, direct traffic, manage ports, print money, repair roads, keep food supplied to the markets, make steel, build rockets, train the police and the army, issue postage stamps or even milk a cow. People provide these services to the ruler through a variety of organizations and institutions. If the people stop providing these skills, the ruler cannot rule.*

From the Centre for Applied NonViolent Action and Strategies (CANVAS) a training organization started by trainers from Otpor. Their website is: http://www.canvasopedia.org

Casino-Free Philadelphia has regularly used this type of power to change policies. For example, as is well-known the public was not allowed to testify at the Pennsylvania Gaming Control Board

(PGCB) meetings for most of its existence. Rather than accept orders from the PGCB chair that said they could not testify, members decided to testify *anyway*.

At a meeting in fall 2007, several members of Casino-Free Philadelphia stood up, one at a time, during the PGCB board meeting. and started testifying. Each one was gaveled down and told to be quiet by the chairwoman. A recess was immediately called. The three members who spoke – unfortunately all the designated spokespeople – were escorted out of the building and told they would not be allowed to return.

When the board reconvened after recess, the chairwoman warned the group not to continue to interrupt. The remainder of the group immediately stood up and attempted to testify. Another recess was called.

Old model of political power

Elites make decisions and those below have no choice but to carry them out

Nonviolent action model of political power:

Through their decision to cooperate or not cooperate those at the bottom hold great power

When the PGCB reconvened again, the group again attempted to speak up. Finally, the chairwoman shut down the entire PGCB meeting rather than allow people to speak.

The result: rather than risk another engagement like that, she allowed the public to speak at the next hearing. Moreover, she initiated a larger shift in policy and now gives time for citizens to speak at several meetings throughout the year.

Mohandas Gandhi said that ultimately the power of people lies in their choice to either cooperate or not cooperate. *Noncooperation* with unjust or wrong authority is the heart of nonviolent direct action.

This flies in the face of the old notion of power which says it flows downwards. Instead, the theory of nonviolent action is that power flows upwards. It's a democratic way of viewing power by seeing that unjust authority is only in place because of the cooperation of all of the layers below it.

That's why people who are oppressed and disenfranchised turn to nonviolent action: it's a step towards empowerment to see how *we* have power – even if we are not powerful politicians, judges, or mayors of a city.

Nonviolent Action Requires Discipline

Members of Casino-Free Philadelphia could not have been successful in that action if they did not carry themselves with respect, show respect to the humanity of the chairwoman while disobeying her orders to be silent, and stay focused on their goals during the action. The *action* is the message in nonviolent action.

Dr. Martin Luther King, Jr. laid out four principles that he used during the civil rights movement. We offer them because when we use *people power* it does require that we act civilly, respectfully, and modeling the highest integrity we can muster:

1) **Define your objectives**. Injustice and violence are everywhere around us. A single campaign or action will not remove it all. One must begin by focusing on a specific injustice; it should be possible to discuss it in fairly simple and clear-cut terms. Decision-making and negotiations during a campaign will be helped immensely if you have defined clearly your short-range objective and your long-range goal.

2) **Be honest and listen well**. Part of your goal is to win your opponent's respect. Conduct yourself in a way which encourages that respect by showing your scrupulous care for truth and justice. A crucial part of nonviolent direct action is the understanding that no one knows the complete truth about the issues at hand. Listening with openness to what your opponents have to say about your campaign is very important in your pursuit of the whole truth. Similarly, listening carefully to those who are struggling at your side helps ensure that the oppression which you are fighting is not replaced by another oppression.

3) **Love your enemies**. No matter how deeply involved in unjust and violent systems some people are, your goal is to break down those systems, not to punish others for wrong-doing. Real justice is established when people refuse to maintain oppressive systems, not when the people in those systems are destroyed. Nonviolence requires a steadfast and conscious willingness to mentally separate respect for all people from disrespect for what some people are doing in a given situation.

4) **Give your opponents a way out**. By using nonviolence, you are showing a kind of strength that overcomes injustice. Avoid self-righteousness with opponents. Recognize their weaknesses, embarrassments and fears. In specific confrontations, as well as in the larger campaign, find a way to let them participate in finding a solution. Give them options to respond to, not non-negotiable demands.

[These principles were first developed in the context of the struggle for civil rights in the U.S. at the request of Dr. Martin Luther King. The present version has been slightly revised for international use by the International Fellowship of Reconciliation]

While many would never even consider *violent* actions, the purpose of clarifying *nonviolent* action is to limit the actions of participants to only those within a framework of disciplined, unified action. Casino-Free Philadelphia uses the following Nonviolent Action Guidelines in all of its direct actions, which are agreed upon by all participants.

In our actions, we will…
✦ bring humor;
✦ adopt a dignified, open and friendly attitude towards anybody we encounter;
✦ demonstrate our creativity in the use of new slogans, songs, and props;
✦ keep our calm, and our eyes on the prize.

In our actions, we will not…
+ bring weapons;
+ use verbal or physical violence;
+ damage property;
+ use drugs or alcohol;
+ hide our identity behind hoods or masks;
+ risk arrest without the required training;
+ run, as it contributes to heightening tensions for everybody.

You getting arrested as part of Casino-Free Philadelphia's Citizens' Document Search. All were charged with "disorderly conduct" and found not guilty.

By setting clear agreed upon guidelines we ensure mutual respect. We know what people around us will and will not do. No provocation will get us off our message.

The Action is the Message

Nonviolent action differs from other forms of protest that are fundamentally about asking for our rights. Strategic nonviolent action is about acting for our rights.

Strategic nonviolent action gives us a basis for mutual trust, greater public support, and a focused channel to highlight injustice.

In strategic nonviolent action our action is our message. For example, Casino-Free Philadelphia ran a direct action campaign called Operation Transparency in the Fall of 2007. The PA Gaming Control Board (PGCB) refused to make public their documents, such as updated site plans and traffic plans. No meaningful public input could be made without access to such basic documents.

The goal was to get the PGCB to stop violating our right to know and release the hidden documents. If they did not release the documents by our December 1 deadline, we vowed to go to their offices in Harrisburg to carry out a "citizens' document search" to make the documents public ourselves. The citizens' document search is a direct action tactic first designed in Ottawa, which we had learned about and brought to our work.

Operation Transparency lasted for two-months, with small media-friendly actions like washing the PGCB's windows to help them become more transparent. After the deadline passed, the documents still had not been released.

Fourteen people carried out the citizens' document search. Two at a time, people stepped forward. They read a "citizens' search warrant" and asked the PGCB to release the documents. They walked forward and were promptly arrested.

All were later found to be "Not Guilty" by a judge who scolded the PGCB's behavior. The judge virtually invited us to return to Harrisburg and do it again if the PGCB did not release the documents and become transparent. Public pressure mounted.

The power of direct action was that our refusal – our noncooperation – resulted in new allies coming to our sides, an increase in dramatic tension for the PGCB, and shed light on the clarity of the wrongfulness of their position.

Without direct action, most pundits would not be citing how bad the PGCB's behavior has been. They would ignore it, just like most ignore most forms of public abuse.

(In fact, while we are on the topic of the media, you can see from their reporting how the media is biased towards a top-down view of power. Their near insistence that the casinos are destined for the riverfront was because they believe power flows from the top. Like politicians, they are not used to power flowing from the bottom. Without us exerting it often enough, why should they see it flow any other way?)

Instead, though, the press consistently reported the action: citizens attempting to get documents that the PGCB was hiding. Several reporters got very involved and began asking the PGCB what was their reason for hiding the documents and why weren't they releasing them.

Asking the PGCB for the documents via a public request would not have done that. (We previously did public requests and were consistently rejected.) Even a rally would not have that result. We needed a media-friendly, savvy way to *highlight the injustice*. The strategic value: *show, don't tell*.

Unlike a strategy which merely asks the government to do the right thing, nonviolent action sees that when people withdraw their consent from an unjust system, it can be forced to give them what they want. The citizens' document search is a classic tactic for that: use our power as citizens to apply power and pressure to our institutions.

It is not reliant upon the current system to give us what we want. It is about using our political power to get it.

In that way, nonviolent direct action is much more powerful than traditional *marches* or *rallies*, which are merely protests asking the government to do the right thing. Nonviolent direct action highlights the injustice by acting in congruence with what we want: we believe we have a right to the documents. Then we won't be satisfied when our rights are denied – we will go take them ourselves.

Nonviolence is thus more than protesting and more than a philosophy of not harming people. We will get into this and more misconceptions about nonviolent action in the next section.

Now that's power to the people.

Misconceptions About Nonviolent Action

In society we are fed myths about nonviolent action. Dr. King, for example, was *not* about service – he was about social change. Creating a "day of service" to honor Dr. King undermines his message of freedom through struggle and suggests change does not require conflict and disagreement. Far from it, he wrote that "I must confess that I am not afraid of the word 'tension.' I have earnestly opposed violent tension, but there is a type of constructive, nonviolent tension which is necessary for growth." (*Letter from Birmingham Jail*, April 16, 1963).

Here are some responses to other common misconceptions about nonviolent action.

You blocking traffic on a highway at a local action using "lock boxes" (see Blockades section).

Myth: Change comes from a superhero who swoops out of the sky to save the day

This myth makes us believe that we have to wait around for the superhero to appear. Because we are not superheroes, we can't change things.

For example, people often think that Rosa Parks was some superhero woman who sparked the whole civil rights movement. Actually, she was a normal woman who took a stand for justice for black folks. Leaders do have a role, but there are many more; the movement is made up of all the people who take a part in it.

Myth: Movements happen like a big explosion – all of a sudden, usually following a crisis

In the Rosa Parks myth, we hear that one day, hard-working Rosa Parks was tired, decided she didn't want to give up her seat on a city bus to a white person, and out of the blue, a movement happened. This gives us the idea that movements explode out of nowhere.

The truth is that Rosa Parks was an experienced civil rights organizer who had been in the movement for awhile. Others before her had refused to give up their seats, but the timing of her action matched the situation.

The groundwork was laid by Rosa Parks along with women like Jo Ann Robinson and the Women's Political Council and pastors like Rev. E. D. Nixon. They had built up mechanisms and relationships so that when Rosa Parks took her action, they were ready with phone numbers to call, resources to make leaflets calling for a boycott, and the framework with which to carry out the bus boycott.

Organizing is the groundwork that makes movements happen.

Adapted from School of Unity & Liberation's Political Education Workshop Manual. (www.schoolofunityandliberation.org).

Myth: Direct action is mostly done by young, white activists in rowdy street actions

Recently the media has created an image of "activists" being people who are angry teenagers and twenty-somethings in the streets yelling and screaming. Some activists fit that stereotype.

But the vast majority of direct action is done by thoughtful citizens trying to make their cities, state, nation or globe a better place. Nonviolent direct action is used in movements ranging from overthrowing dictators (e.g. Serbia, Ukraine, Ghana, Philippines), environmental justice (e.g. Greenpeace, Sierra Club), civil rights, women's rights, gay/lesbian rights, and many more.

If you took a look at US history overall you would find that a wide range was done by laborers struggling for freedom of speech, the concept of the weekend, or minimum wage. Today it is being used by groups from Iraq Veterans Against the War to ADAPT – a disability rights group fighting for humane treatment of people with disabilities to, of course, Casino-Free Philadelphia.

Contradiction to Other Myths and Misconceptions

1) Nonviolent action has nothing to do with passivity, submissiveness, and cowardice; just as in violent action, these concepts must first be rejected and overcome.

2) Nonviolent action is not to be equated with verbal or purely psychological persuasion, although it may use action to induce psychological pressures for attitude change; non-violent action, instead of words, is a sanction and a technique of struggle involving the use of social, economic, and political power, and the matching of forces in conflict.

3) Nonviolent action does not depend on the assumption that people are inherently "good"; the potentialities of people for both "good" and "evil" are recognized, including the extremes of cruelty and inhumanity.

4) People using nonviolent action do not have to be pacifists or saints; nonviolent action has been predominantly and successfully practiced by "ordinary" people.

5) Success with nonviolent action does not require (thought it may be helped by) shared standards and principles, a high degree of community of interest, or a high degree of psychological closeness between the contending groups; this is because when efforts to produce voluntary change fail, coercive nonviolent measures may be employed.

6) Nonviolent action is at least as much of a Western phenomenon as an Eastern one; indeed, it is probably more Western, if one takes into account the widespread use of strikes and boycotts in the labor movement and the noncooperation struggles of subordinated nationalities.

7) In nonviolent action there is no assumption that the opponent will refrain from using violence against nonviolent actionists; the technique is designed to operate against violence when necessary.

8) There is nothing in nonviolent action to prevent it from being used for both "good" and "bad" causes although the social consequences of its use for a "bad" cause may differ considerably from the consequences of violence used for the same cause.

9) Nonviolent action is not limited to domestic conflicts within a democratic system; it has been widely used against dictatorial regimes, foreign occupations, and even against totalitarian systems.

10) Nonviolent action does not always take longer to produce victory than violent struggle would. In a variety of cases nonviolent struggle has won objectives in a very short time -- in as little as a few days. The time taken to achieve victory depends on diverse factors -- primarily on the strength of the nonviolent actionists.

What nonviolent action is

Nonviolent action is a generic term covering dozens of specific methods of protest, noncooperation, and intervention, in all of which the actionists conduct the conflict by doing -- or refusing to do -- certain things without using physical violence. As a technique, therefore, nonviolent action is not passive. It is not inaction. It is action that is nonviolent.

The issue at stake will vary. Frequently it may be a political one -- between political groups, for or against a government, or on rare occasions, between governments (as in imposition of embargoes or resistance to occupation). It may also be economic or social or religious. The scale and level of the conflict will also vary. It may be limited to a neighborhood, a city, or a particular section of the society; it may at other times range over a large area of a country or convulse a whole nation. Less often, more than one country and government may be involved. Whatever the issue, however, and whatever the scale of the conflict, nonviolent action is a technique by which people who reject passivity and submission, and who see struggle as essential, can wage their conflict without violence. Nonviolent action is not an attempt to avoid or ignore conflict. It is one response to the problem of how to act in politics, especially how to wield power effectively.

Source: Gene Sharp, The Politics of Nonviolent Action, (3 Vols..), Boston: Porter Sargent, 1973. The article was originally published by the Albert Einstein Institution, 50 Church Street, Cambridge, MA 02138. tel:(617)876 0311 fax:(617)876 0387, Email: einstein@igc.apc.org

Introduction to Blockades

Nonviolent direct action is made up of hundreds of different tactics: citizens' document searches, sit-ins, marches, debate-ins, public filibuster of meetings, and many more. Blockades are a specific tactic for nonviolent direct action.

Blockades have been used by groups in a range of situations to stop harmful development. One of the most experienced groups on blockades is the environmentalist movement, which uses blockades to protect old growth trees from being cut down. Their strategy is often to protect the trees long enough for legal solutions to be found to permanently protect the trees.

But blockades have been used by citizens for other purposes. For years people in wheelchairs have blockaded entrances to buildings or buses, protesting the discrimination they face by being unable to enter non-wheelchair accessible buses or buildings. More often than not, they have fulfilled their goals. Citizens regularly use blockades to stop or slow-down the building of harmful development.

Types of Blockades: Soft and Hard

Soft blockades only use people's bodies. This is the literal image of standing in front of a bulldozer. Hard blockades, however, add the use of gear such as u-locks. Hard blockades tend to be used when the goal is to occupy a particular place for an extended period of time. Some hard blockades have lasted months; similarly, some soft blockades have lasted for weeks. Soft blockades tend to be quicker for police to remove from a location; but they also are safer for participants and tend to be seen as less radical.

Soft Blockades (no gear)

The image of people joining together to blockade a location communicates a powerful visual image of nonviolent civil disobedience: people are physically putting their bodies on the line to stop an injustice. Doing a human blockade without gear is a flexible way to hold space and can be deployed nearly anywhere. Since it doesn't take a lot of resources, a non-gear blockade is easy to "spring" on the target and allows greater options for different levels of participation and arrest risk. (When someone is removed or needs to leave, it is possible to re-group and continue the blockade.)

However, blockades without gear don't have great "staying power" since they rely on personal strength to hold the formation. Unless you have an incredibly large number of people, very good media and/or are mixed in with folks using gear, you can expect to be removed fairly quickly, if the police decide to do so. The power of human blockades is often more emotional and visual.

Specific techniques for soft blockades include linking with each other in various formations, including (but not limited to):

✦ Milling – no linking but people just milling around a site
✦ Linking Arms

- ✦ Linking Legs
- ✦ Back to Back
- ✦ Circle
- ✦ Theatre – people enacting an image

You using an example of a hard blockade to protest money flowing to support the Burmese military dictatorship.

Hard Blockades (with gear)

Blockades that incorporate gear can help a group to hold their ground for a much longer period of time and communicate a high level of commitment to the action. There are many different types of gear that can be incorporated – let your imagination go!

However, the risks involved with the decision to use gear should be weighed carefully. Using gear opens up a new realm of safety and need for training: some devices increase the risk of injury simply by design. Thorough preparation for a gear-based blockade is essential. If you don't have the training, experience, and support to do a gear-based blockade correctly, it is better not to do it.

Examples of hard blockades include (but are not limited to):

- ✦ U-lock – using a u-lock to lock your body to some immovable object
- ✦ Motorcycle cables and chains – using hard chains to lock yourself to an object and provide greater flexibility
- ✦ Lock-boxes – PVC pipes with metal inside so that people can hold hands together.

Risk in Blockading

Nonviolent Direct Action and Civil Disobedience always involve some level of risk. Some aspects of risk are within your control, and some are not. Police and public reaction to a particular action is never 100% predictable. By thinking through your action and the context in which it will take place, you can develop some scenarios to help you predict how things will go.

Before engaging in blockades, you should attend a full training session on the specific blockade you will be using. Plus, organizers will be responsible for full action planning, looking at various options.

Some ways to reduce risk include:

Be strategic. Make sure your tactics are informed by the vision, goals and strategy. Don't think in terms of "soft" vs. "hard" or "more radical." Instead, think in terms of what is appropriate for the goals, strategy, tone, message risk, level of escalation, etc.

Get help. Take advantage of the experience of others, through training, or on-site support. Everyone does it for the first time once. And the more experience you have, the more responsibility you have to support others in an appropriate way.

Start simple. Build up. Don't deploy all your technology at once. Leave room to escalate during the action, if that is appropriate.

All roles are important. A good support team is essential. People who are not wanting to risk being part of a blockade are needed to help out other logistics, paying attention to safety, talking to media, and more.

Scout. Scout. Scout. Spend a lot of time getting to know your location.

Practice. Over and over. Then practice some more. The more you practice, the safer you will be and the more effective your action will be.

Make a Plan B....and C, D & E, if you think you might need it (or not!).

Plan a media strategy and execute. Make sure your message gets out and that your action logic is as transparent as possible. Don't let communications be an afterthought.

Eliminate unnecessary risk. Make your action as safe as it can be to achieve your goals.

Dress for success. Make sure that your appearance helps carry the tone you want to set for your action. Dress comfortably. Have your support people around with layers, if it gets cold.

Stay hydrated. Make sure your support people can get water to you, if you can not use your hands.

Be Creative. Have Fun.

Adapted from forthcoming blockades training manual from The Ruckus Society, an organization committed to creative, strategic, nonviolent direct actions (www.Ruckus.org).

Why People Risk Nonviolent Action

Statements from citizens engaged in Citizens' Document Search

Rev. Jesse Brown

The community has been left out of the process of being able to have a meaningful input into the casinos that may be coming to our particular communities. All this revenue people think they will be getting from these things gets nullified real quickly when you start talking about the social issues casinos bring. Their lack of transparency is harming us and our communities.

Marj Rosenblum

I am from East Passyunk. The unique character of the many neighborhoods of our city would be undermined by putting Casinos near any of our unique neighborhoods. As a teacher I abhor the inherent lesson of gambling i.e., the emphasis on luck as a way to make money instead of hard work. I feel pity for us as a nation that we feel the only way we can fund our schools or take care of our senior citizens is by lotteries and gambling.

Meredith Warner

I am willing to search the office of the PGCB because I believe that I have the right to know exactly what the slots operators have planned for my neighborhood. The people of Philadelphia are being forced to play "good neighbor" with a secretive, outside, wealthy industry. Without a true understanding of the impact of a slots parlor just 4 short blocks from my home, how can I really assess or prepare for it? The state should be protecting me from the gambling industry, not protecting the gambling industry from the citizens of the state!

Daniel Hunter Article: Let's Become Creatively Maladjusted

For over a year I have been involved in fighting casinos and the two slot locations in Philly's neighborhoods. Many have told me that they have seen a deep sense of integrity, creativity, and boldness in this movement. I hope some of that may be true. This casino fight is about more than just casinos -- it is about intervening on the near constant barrage of public abuse by public and elected officials.

I'll give you one recent example. After seventeen months of refusing the allow public testimony to the board, yesterday a dozen Philadelphia residents, one by one, stood up and attempted to testify at the PA Gaming Control Board hearing. They cited the Sunshine Act, the PA Constitution, and just plain ol' democracy.

We were rebuffed by Chairwoman Mary Collins saying that she would not take public testimony. But residents persisted. After three residents were escorted out, others kept attempting to testify. Some tried to speak about how SugarHouse and Foxwoods both lied to the Board in order to get their licenses or shared the dramatic stories of public and City Council pressure.

But unlike Arizona, Illinois, New Jersey or other states, PA decided to keep the public out and gaveled the entire meeting to a close. The Pennsylvania Gaming Control Board decided they would rather shut down their meeting than allow the public to speak.

Unfortunately, it is not just a common experience for those of us engaged in this issue, but an experience shared broadly in Philadelphia. Nearly every Philadelphian has their own story about how their voice was kept out, or how elected officials told them it's impossible, or how public officials used insider deals to advance their own cause to the detriment of the city.

Corruption and insider deals are stifling us, limiting our innovation and vision, and keeping cycles of violence and depression well-alive in our city. Instead of an inspirational plan for the riverfront, like other cities have and are implementing, the corrupt casino process has led us to two slots barns, unwanted by neighborhoods. According to recent studies these developments will actually destroy more local jobs than they create.

But I believe we need to move beyond just calling this corruption. Because corruption is what the powerful elites do with each other, at the exclusion of the public. "Corruption" does not describe our role.

What we are witnessing is public abuse. Unlike private abuse it is not behind closed doors, it is in the open where everyone can see. It often shows up as government policy. It is leaders telling the public they cannot speak. It is the City making deals with those with money to evict neighbors who have lived in their homes for generations. It is L&I using their process to make people afraid of talking about what a political tool they are. It is the City Planning Commission having a collective zero years of planning experience and operating purely on politics. It is making developers jump through a million hoops to build in this city when a clean, transparent process would be better for all.

This abuse of the public leads to deep cynicism and distrust. Nonvoters rightly ask: why vote if it's one corruption option or another? Our response has been to act more boldly, to publicly speak out, to shake off shackles of fear, and to take our demands beyond the ballot box.

Dr. Martin Luther King, Jr. called this being "creatively maladjusted." He said, "It is good certainly declaring that destructive maladjustment should be eradicated. But on the other hand, I am sure that we all recognize that there are some things in our society, some things in our world to which we should never be adjusted. There are some things that we must always be maladjusted to if we are to be people of good will."

Instead, he argued for being creatively maladjusted.

In Philadelphia we grow used to public abuse. Too often, we accept and silently watch while it happens. We commonly perpetuate it by discouraging others from speaking their minds. Many people of good will have said to me, "Casinos are a done deal, don't fight them." But that's their fear and internalized acceptance of public abuse. If we choose to say no, we can keep hope alive, as our movement has continually shown. Accepting the abuse and teaching others to accept the abuse is antithetical to the direction we want to go. Telling others not to stand up for themselves participates in the public abuse. Saying nothing does, too.

Creative maladjustment encourages us to stand up against the ways the City and State abuse us. It can be simple. If you want to speak at a public meeting, do it whether they've said you can or not. If you want to ask a question at City Council, do it even if it interrupts the flow. It's not to be disruptive, but to implement the vision of a transparent, open city. If we don't take responsibility for corruption, it will continue to abuse us.

And if you see one of us doing it, even if you disagree on our point, publicly defend our right to say it. That's why I'm proud to be one of those escorted out by the Gaming Control Board. I was personally scared but even more honored to be with others who joined us. And while the Board made the wrong decision by shutting down its meeting and therefore allowing nobody to speak, if we persist as a city we will earn their respect. Afterall, as long as we act like victims we will not earn an end to corruption and public abuse.

The PGCB, of course, eventually allowed public testimony having regular sessions where the public can speak. Casino-Free Philadelphia was the first such public group to testify in over seventeen months of being locked out. Written by Daniel Hunter in September 2007 and republished in several newspapers and CFP's website.

Why Training for Nonviolent Direct Action?

[Casino-Free Philadelphia requires that all participants involved in its direct actions undergo careful training. Here are a few of the reasons why, written by expert-in-the-field George Lakey, who has offered multiple trainings to CFP.]

To deepen participants' understanding of the issues. Dr. Martin Luther King, Jr., initiated in 1968 a "Poor People's Campaign" to reduce poverty in the U.S. Teachers and students at the Martin Luther King School of Social Change designed workshops to explore racism, poverty, and direct action to prepare participants to join the campaign. People who have been victimized by injustice may have a limited (though vivid) understanding of oppression, and need a "bigger picture" to enable them to struggle more effectively for change.

To prepare participants psychologically for the struggle. The Pinochet regime in Chile depended, as dictatorships do, on fear to maintain its control. In the 1980s a group committed to nonviolent struggle encouraged people to face their fears directly in a three-step process: small group training sessions in living rooms, followed by small, "hit-and-run" nonviolent actions, followed by de-briefing sessions. By teaching people to control their fear, trainers intended to prepare the way for the fall of the dictatorship.

To develop group discipline, morale, and solidarity for more effective action. In 1991 members of ACT-UP (a militant group protesting U.S. AIDS policy) were beaten up by Philadelphia police during a demonstration. The police were found guilty of unnecessary force and the city paid damages, but ACT-UP members realized they could reduce the chance of future brutality by acting in a more united and nonviolent way. Before their next major action they invited a trainer to conduct a civil disobedience workshop; they clarified the strategic question of nonviolence and then role-played possible scenarios. The result: a high-spirited, unified and effective civil disobedience action.

The power of nonviolent action is related to the group morale of the participants. Training workshops are often designed to assist a group to make a tighter bond, or even for strangers to develop a new sense of group spirit. In 1964 the Student Nonviolent Coordinating Committee (SNCC) and other civil rights organizations called upon college students from all over the U.S. to register voters and organize freedom schools in "Mississippi Summer." Two week-long training workshops were held in succession in Ohio, each for 400-500 students; community-building was a major focus of the training. Midway in the second workshop the news broke that two of the participants in the first workshop were already found murdered in Mississippi. Despite the almost palpable fear among the students, nearly all of them stayed with the community, completed the training, and went to Mississippi.

Solidarity issues can come up at many points in preparation for action. Trainers can:

- introduce the option of "jail solidarity:" noncooperation with the system in order to protect all members of the group and get demands met;
- sensitize participants to the possibility of "special treatment" by authorities of people of color, non-citizens, juveniles, gays, people with AIDS, etc.;
- stimulate dialogue on the tactic of refusing bail after arrest as having classist implications;
- make sure support people are affirmed (not only those who have been jailed or beaten);
- ask how the action will remain accessible to people with disabilities;
- introduce the notion of violence as going beyond physical force to include poverty, racism, sexism, etc.

To revise and develop strategy. In 1973 the New Zealand anti-apartheid movement was divided on how to protest the scheduled rugby tour of the white South African rugby team. Three workshops were scheduled with a visiting trainer both to learn more about how other social movements have used nonviolent action and also to develop their own strategy and tactics. Top leadership of the movement participated. The result: a strategy (and coordination among leadership) which led to the government canceling the South African tour.

One way that workshops support smarter strategy is through increased understanding of the opponent and other parties to the conflict. Many of the strategic mistakes made by nonviolent movements have been caused by lack of understanding of where the other players "are coming from." Through strategy games and other training tools, participants stretch their knowledge base and their imaginations.

To revise and clarify tactics. For success nonviolent strategies usually require tactical flexibility; campaigns often need creative and bold tactical maneuver. Through training participants learn the overall goals of the action, important logistical and legal information, and share guidelines so people know what to expect from each other. Often in the workshops themselves "affinity groups" are created, which become the fundamental action units or teams.

You joining the Boston Tea Party, an example of nonviolent direct action, to protest taxes and unfair treatment by the British Crown.

These elements of training set the tone for the action and optimize the chance of tactical flexibility within the larger strategic framework.

To prepare participants for decisions they need to make. Although strategies and tactics are chosen by the organization or campaign, some decisions must be made by individuals -- for example, whether to risk arrest. Workshops provide legal information, set up support systems for notifying families etc., and assist individuals to decide how to participate in the action.

To develop understanding of the dynamics of nonviolent struggle. In 1989 the United Mine Workers of America decided to go beyond a conventional strike in its dispute with the Pittston Coal Company, launching a nonviolent civil disobedience campaign. The union called together 50 field staff who would be the "lieutenants" in the struggle for a training workshop. While roleplaying, the staffers acted on the widely-held belief that direct action is a contest with police to hold "turf" -- for example, the road where the coal trucks drive. Through repeated roleplays and careful de-briefing, the staffers learned that nonviolent methods operate through dynamics which are more political than material -- that power is too complex to reduce to who physically occupies what at a particular moment. The coal miners went on to win their campaign against heavy odds, and set a new standard for labor action in the U.S.

Scholars and researchers in nonviolent action, social movements, group dynamics, and related fields can regard training as a "transmission belt" for conveying knowledge to the field for application and feedback. They can also can use workshops as places to learn from activists and generate new hypotheses.

To build skills for applying nonviolent action. In Haiti a "hit squad" abducted a young man just outside the house where a foreign peace team was staying. The team immediately intervened and, although surrounded by twice their number of guards with weapons, succeeded nonviolently in saving the man from a hanging.

Successful campaigns and interventions need more than sound strategy and high morale: they also need specific skills -- which are rarely taught in schools! For example: from the independence campaigns of colonial India of the 1940s to the civil rights marches in Northern Ireland of the 1960s to the anti-apartheid struggle in South Africa of the 1980s, movement leaders have faced the challenge of violence erupting, inviting repression, and dividing the movement. (Often agents will even be hired to stimulate violence, as the British did in India and the FBI did in the U.S. movement against the Vietnam War.) A specific skill for such situations is marshalling (also called peacekeeping), and many movements have trained marshals with specific skills to handle such incidents.

To build alliances across movement lines. In Seattle a workshop drew striking workers from the Greyhound bus company and members of the militant AIDS protest group Act Up. The workshop reduced the prejudice each group had about the other, and led some participants to support each others' struggles.

One block to uniting potential allies can be the lack of common experience; another can be lack of common understanding of strategy and tactics. These blocks as well as prejudice can be reduced through action training workshops which bring potential allies together.

To increase democracy within the movement. In the 1970s the Movement for a New Society developed a pool of training tools and designs which it shared with the grassroots movement against nuclear power. The anti-nukes movement went up against local electrical companies, and some of the largest corporations in America, and the federal government itself -- and won. The movement delayed construction, which raised costs, and planted so many seeds of doubt in the public mind about safety that the near melt-down of the Three Mile Island plant brought millions of people to the movement's point of view. The industry's goal of 1000 nuclear plants evaporated. The environmentalists succeeded without creating a national structure around a charismatic leader and even without centralized leadership, because they learned the tools of shared leadership and democratic decision-making, through countless workshops, practice, and feedback.

One way to reduce democracy is for leadership to monopolize skills and knowledge. Training, by contrast, spreads the skills and knowledge around, making possible more broadly shared leadership.

Extracted from George Lakey, Why Training for Nonviolent Action as printed in *International Journal of Nonviolence*, Volume II, Number 1.

How to De-escalate

Conducting higher risk actions, such as a blockade, requires preparation. We encourage all participants to go through direct action training beforehand including a full session on de-escalation.

De-escalation may have different goals: ensuring physical safety of all participants, reducing the likelihood of violence from your own people, keeping a relaxed media presence, or allowing yourself to stay on the site longer. In any case, every situation has its own dynamic and is unique: there is no formula for reacting to a hostile situation. When entering an action, it is best to think through possible difficult situations and be prepared ahead of time.

Below are some behaviors that are successful in hostile situations to de-escalate the situation.

1. **REMAIN CALM** — Avoid panicking and hectic reactions. Try not to provoke reflex reactions. Find out about your own means to develop inner strength and calmness and to maintain it in threatening situations. When faced with a violent situation take your time to become conscious of yourself.

2. **BECOME ACTIVE** — Do not become paralyzed by fear. It is better to do something small to change the situation than contemplate big actions that you might not be able to do. Very often there are technical possibilities to de-escalating or prevent more violence (e.g., emergency brakes in trains). The military reports that people who handle crisis situations best are those who do not freeze, who do anything.

You practicing good de-escalation skills.

3. **TRY TO ESTABLISH COMMUNICATION WITH THE AGGRESSOR** — If someone is being aggressive, keep an open body language and communication with them. Look for common ground that moves away from the current situation (e.g. introduce yourself).

4. **LOOK FOR HELP: ENLIST ALLIES** — In this action, you are not alone. However, instead of appealing to a large crowd of people for help, make eye contact with one person and ask them for help. Others will feel encouraged by your direct demand for help. Trust your gut in selecting someone to individually ask. And, if that person does not work, try the next person until you find an ally (don't give up!)

5. **WALK AWAY** — If after trying different ways, you cannot find a successful way to de-escalate the situation, it is perfectly okay to walk away. It is better that you are safe and nobody is hurt, then someone does something they later will regret.

Originally written by Hagen Berndt (Kurve-Wustrow) as an adaptation of Milan's list of rules Adapted by Daniel Hunter, Training for Change (www.TrainingForChange.org) and director of Casino-Free Philadelphia (www.CasinoFreePhila.org).

Movement Action Plan

Part 1: A Map for Our Course

[In our movement we have often referred to the Movement Action Plan. Here is a more full description than we have printed before, extracted from Grassroots and Nonprofit Leadership.*]*

The rich history of social movements means that we do not entirely have to make it up as we go along. We can learn from what worked and what didn't, and the lessons from movements then inform the choices we make as we steer our organizations. The authors have learned a lot about the life cycle of movements from long-time organizer Bill Moyer, who worked with Dr. King on the staff of the Southern Christian Leadership Conference, was a major strategist for the anti-nuclear power movement, and assisted a variety of other movements and organizations. From his study and experience Bill has created a model of how successful movements achieve their goals, the Movement Action Plan (MAP).

MAP is a development model; that is, it shows how movements evolve, step by step. Just as we think about human beings with a development model (infancy, adolescence, middle age), so also it helps us think about our social change work to have a framework of stages.

Of course MAP is only one way of looking at social movements. We have found it useful, especially in understanding how to steer an organization through the ups and downs of a cause. Bill has kindly allowed us to summarize his model for this book, and we recommend that you read it with the history of your issue in mind.

First, a word about models. A model airplane is a simplified version of the real thing. You wouldn't want to fly in it, but it gives you an idea of what it's like and can even by useful for certain tests. An architect often builds a model of a building before the real thing goes up with all its complications. Like all models, MAP is a simplification of a very complex reality, and helps us to face reality with more clarity and perspective.

Bill's model shows us how the development stages of a successful movement relate to public opinion, so before we get into the internal life of the movement, we'll take a quick overview of the public. Before there is a social movement around a certain injustice, the body politic seems to be asleep. The toxic waste is being routinely dumped, for example, with office holders looking the other way and public opinion preoccupied with other things. This is stage one.

Then stress builds and the body politic wakes up. In stages two, three, and four, more and more of the public notices what's going on, and the office holders get busy reassuring the public that they are taking care of the problem and it's OK to go back to sleep. In each of stages two, three, and four, the movement's growth is in a different place.

By stages five and six the majority of the public agrees with the movement that change is needed (the war should be stopped, or nuclear power is too dangerous, for example). There's a debate though, about possible alternatives. Stage five is a letdown time for activists, and can be tricky; some movements just die in this stage instead of moving ahead to success.

At last comes success, in stages seven and eight. Many office holders are proclaiming that they really wanted these changes all along, while some of the holdouts are being voted out of office. New groups are spinning off the main reform movement to start the process all over again. Most of the public is glad to stop talking about civil rights, or Vietnam, or nuclear power, and go back to their individual concerns (which, from an activist's point of view, looks like going back to sleep!).

Stage One: Business as Usual
Only a relatively few people care about the issue at this point, and they form small groups to support each other. Their objective: to get people thinking. They do their best to spread the word and often try small action projects.

Stage Two: Failure of Established Channels
A major reason why most of the public does not inform itself and act on an injustice is that people think (or hope) that established structures are taking care of it. "Surely the government is watching out for the safety of our ground water supply." "The government is researching AIDS." "Corporate scientists know which chemicals are dangerous in our workplace and which are not."

In this stage the small groups challenge the established channels. They often do research, or get victims of injustice to file formal complaints. They may sue governmental agencies, or use any opportunities to appeal that exist in the regulations. Usually the activists lose at this stage, but it is very important that they take these steps. Stage two is essential for change, since large-scale participation will not happen as long as people believe in the established channels. In fact, you'll find that, by stage two, polls show fifteen to twenty percent of public opinion is leaning toward a change.

Stage Three: Ripening Conditions/Education and Organizing
Now the pace picks up considerably because many people who earlier did not want to listen become interested. The movement creates many new groups who work on this issue, largely through education. The groups send speakers to religious groups and union halls; they do marches through their communities; they hold house meetings and news conferences. Much of the content of what they say is refuting powerholders' claims: "People start pollution; people can stop it," "Radiation is not really all that bad for you," "Plenty is already being done to prevent AIDS." This stage can take a very long time or a short time, depending on many things, but constant outreach, through education and forming new groups, is essential for the movement to take off. By now, polls show twenty to thirty percent agree that there is a problem or an injustice.

Stage Four: Takeoff
This stage is usually initiated by a trigger event, a dramatic happening that puts a spotlight on the problem, sparking wide public attention and concern. Sometimes the trigger event is created by

the movement. In 1963 the Southern Christian Leadership Conference, headed by Dr. Martin Luther King, Jr., focused on Birmingham, Alabama, in a direct action campaign which filled the jails and highlighted the evils of segregation with vivid pictures of police dogs and fire hoses. The Birmingham campaign triggered a national and international response, which resulted in the passage of major civil rights legislation.

Sometimes the trigger event just happens, like the near meltdown at the Three Mile Island nuclear reactor in 1979. Three Mile Island (TMI) precipitated massive nonviolent protest and propelled many new people into activity. Previous movement growth had been substantial, but TMI triggered a crisis atmosphere that brought depth and breadth to the movement. MAP shows that the takeoff stage needs the preparation of stages two and three. Nuclear power provides an example we can explore.

Many years before TMI, the Fermi nuclear plant in the city of Detroit nearly melted down. A disaster similar or worse than TMI threatened then, yet there was no social crisis and spurt of anti-nuclear organizing. Why? Because there was no previous social movement challenging the normal channels (stage two) and no education and organizing (stage three). An event becomes a trigger event when a movement has first done its homework.

Because of the high media profile in this stage, many people associate social change with stage four. Often one or more large coalitions form at this time. Celebrities join the movement, the powerholders are shocked by the new opposition and publicity and try to discredit the movement, and polls show forty to sixty percent of the public say they oppose the injustice or current policies. Activists often unrealistically expect a quick victory at this point and work around the clock. Long rambling meetings occur in which new people come and try to make decisions without the necessary procedures in place. The issue is seen in isolation from other issues.

The objectives of stage four are to build and coordinate a new grassroots movement and to win over public opinion. Part of winning the public is connecting the demands of the movement with widely held values (like freedom, fairness, or democracy).

Stage Five: Perception of Failure
There's an old phrase: "Two steps forward, one step back." Stage five is the step back, in the perception of many activists. Numbers are down at demonstrations, the media pay less attention, and the policy changes have not yet been won. The powerholders' official line is, "The movement failed." The media focuses on splits in the movement and especially on activities which offend public sensibilities.

It is the excitement and lack of planning on stage four that create the sense of failure in stage five. By believing that success is at hand, activists can become disillusioned and despairing when they realize they aren't there yet. Hoping to recapture the excitement and confidence of stage four, some groups create Rambo-style actions of anger and violence or become a permanent counterculture sect that is isolated and ineffective.

Fortunately, a great many activists do not become discouraged, or if they do, accept it as part of the process. They treat it like rafters on a river who most of all love excitement of the white water, but also accept the slow times in between.

Smart strategists lay out strategic, achievable and measurable objectives, and smart movements celebrate them as they achieve them along the way. The powerholders may try to crush the movement through repression at this point, even if they have felt constrained before by a civil liberties tradition. Even repression, however, can sometimes be responded to in the spirit of celebration, as a symptom of achievement.

Stage Six: Winning Over the Majority

In this stage the movement transforms. Protest in crisis gives way to long-term struggle with powerholders. The goal is to win majority opinion. Many new groups, which include people who previously were not active, are formed. The new groups do grassroots education and action. The issue shows up in electoral campaigns, and some candidates get elected on this platform. Broader coalitions become possible, and mainstream institutions expand their own programs to include the issue.

Until stage six, much of the movement's energy was focused on opposition (to toxic waste, to war, to homelessness, etc.). In stage six, sixty to seventy-five percent of the public agrees on a need for change. There is no a vast audience ready to think about alternatives to existing policies, and the smart movement offers some. Mainstream institutions can be helpful at this point. One example comes from the anti-Vietnam War movement: universities responded to stage four with peace studies courses and departments, and during stage six many of the scholars involved began thinking about alternatives to the war system.

You using a metaphoric image – the oil barrel – as a prop in your blockade protesting the Iraq war.

The powerholders are not passive. They try to discredit and disrupt the movement, insist there is no positive alternative, promote bogus reforms, and sometimes create crisis events to scare the public. The powerholders themselves also become more split in this period.

The dangers of this stage are: national organizations and staff may dominate the movement and reduce grassroots energy; reformers may compromise too much or try to deliver the movement into the hands of politicians; a belief may spread that the movement is failing because it has not yet succeeded.

Stage Seven: Achieving Alternatives

Stages seven and eight could be called managing success. They are tricky, however, because the game isn't over until it's over. In stage seven, the goals are to recognize the movement's success (not as easy as it sounds!), to empower activists and their organizations to act effectively, to achieve a major objective or demand, and to achieve that demand within the framework of a paradigm shift — a new model or way of thinking about the issue.

Goals or demands need to be consistent with a different way of looking at things: a new framework or paradigm. If a civil rights movement simply demands some changes of personnel in government, industry, or schools, it will get more women, people of color or lesbians and gays occupying functions that continue business as usual, including policies which oppress women, people of color, and gays. Social movements are usually much more creative than that, and project new visions of how things can be. A successful social movement, therefore, can gain objectives that, although grudgingly yielded by the powerholders, introduce a new way of operating and of being.

Stage seven is a long process, not an event. The struggle shifts in this stage from opposing present policies to creating dialogue about which alternatives to adopt. The movement will have differences within itself about alternatives, and different groups will market different alternatives to the public. The central powerholders will try their last gambits, including study commissions and bogus alternatives, and then be forced to change their policies, have their policies defeated, or lose office.

It's not unusual for another trigger event to come along (the Chernobyl nuclear meltdown) or be created (the 1965 Selma freedom march in the civil rights movement), which gives increased energy to the cause and wins over still more allies.

Each movement needs to develop an endgame which makes sense in terms of its own goals and situation. The fight against nuclear power is an example of change in which there was never a showdown in the United States Congress. Instead, the movement created enough obstacles in the U.S. market to result in a de facto moratorium on new plants, partly by showing them to be unacceptably costly.

Stage Eight: Consolidation and Moving On
The movement leaders need to protect and extend the successes achieved. The movement also becomes midwife to other social movements. We saw growing out of the 1960s civil rights movement the student movement, the anti-Vietnam war movement, the farmworkers union, the women's movement, the American Indian movement, and others. The long-term focus of stage eight is to achieve a paradigm shift, to change the cultural framework.

The paradigm shift the civil rights movement initiated is still a major part of the U.S. agenda thirty-five years later: diversity as a positive value. In the 1950s, difference was shunned and feared. The rule was to conform. Even rock and roll was attacked as "a communist plot," because it was different from prevailing pop music. Ethnic minorities were taught to be as White and middle class as possible to fit in — that was their only hope (and not a large one) for acceptance. The momentum of the civil rights movement and the movements it midwived continues today as an often intense struggle to see difference differently and to create the structures and processes that make diversity a strength in building community.

While the movement is consolidating its gains and dealing with backlash from those who never were persuaded, the powerholders are adapting to new policies and conditions and often claiming the movement's success as their own. At the same time, they may fail to carry out agreements, fail to pass sufficient new legislation, or weaken the impact of new structures by appointing people who are resistant to the change. A major pitfall awaiting activists in stage eight, therefore, is neglecting to make sure of institutional follow-through.

In this stage, the movement not only can celebrate the specific changes it has gained, but also can notice and celebrate the larger ripple effect it has in other aspects of society and even in other societies. The U.S. movement against nuclear weapons was inspired by the mass occupations of construction sites by German environmentalists. On this shrinking planet, we get to learn from and inspire each other internationally.

If You Think You're Lost, Check the Map

The course of the river is winding, and sometimes it divides and goes in unexpected directions. Maybe you feel lost; maybe someone wants you to feel lost. Notice that powerholders generally continue the policy you are campaigning against, even while they secretly are laying plans to announce new policies and to prepare the public to accept them. They deliberately hide their defeat from the public, understandably. When you give in to discouragement, you are accepting their definition of the situation. You don't need to — a strategic framework enables you to define the situation.

The last four years of the anti-Vietnam War movement provide our example. The U.S. government stepped up its bombing of Vietnam, exceeding all the bombing of Europe in World War II, and publicly stated its commitment to continuing the war indefinitely. This visible, aggressive policy depressed most antiwar activists, who thought that their ten years of effort had been wasted.

Activists did not know that the U.S. government was at the same time quietly beginning to give up the war. The United States began peace talks in Paris with the North Vietnamese. It then gave in to two key movement demands: withdrawing U.S. troops from Vietnam and ending the military draft. Movement activists saw these moves as irrelevant plots that undercut the movement's opposition. In the last years, the anti-Vietnam War movement became totally depressed. Then, suddenly, the war ended. Former government officials have acknowledged that the movement was extremely effective in ending the war. To activists at the time, however, it felt just the opposite!

You're likely to find yourself beached on that same shore with those activists unless you have a stable strategic framework to use when your work seems discouraging. Check out the MAP — it may keep you going long enough to win!

From Grassroots and Nonprofit Leadership: A Guide for Organizations in Changing Times, by Berit Lakey, George Lakey, Rod Napier and Janice Robinson, pages 17-25). Read more about the Movement Action Plan in Bill Moyer's book, Doing Democracy, available from the Training for Change website (www.TrainingForChange.org).

Part 2: Checking The Map – An Analysis of our Current Moment

[From time to time we have used Bill Moyer's Movement Action Plan to analyze the stages of the anti-casino movement. The Movement Action Plan (MAP) is a sketch of how social movements move through time. Social movements, like a growing child, have some natural developmental steps. Instead of fighting some of the struggles with each stage, it's best to acknowledge that each stage has its own strengths and its own weaknesses. Written by Daniel Hunter and updated July 2008.]

To review, the stages of the Movement Action Plan are:

Stage 1: Normal times. *Problem exists, but is not on social or political agenda. Movement uses official channels, demonstrations are small and rare.*

Stage 2: Prove failure of official institutions. *New wave of grassroots opposition begins. Movement uses official system to prove it violates widely-held values (e.g. analyses of the poor casino choices)*

Stage 3: Ripening conditions. *Tensions build. Rising grassroots discontent with conditions, institutions, and powerholders. Movement: grassroots groups grow in number and size. Small nonviolent actions begin (e.g. Operation Transparency)*

Stage 4: Take-off. *Trigger event puts spotlight on problem that violates widely- held values, sparking public attention and upset. Massive non-violent actions and a new grassroots-based social movement (e.g. No Way Without Our Say petition drive, Philly's Ballot Box)*

Stage 5: Perception of failure. *Movement: numbers down at demonstrations, less media, long-range goals not met. Unrealistic hopes of quick success are unmet (e.g. much of last summer)*

Stage 6: Majority Public Opinion. *Movement transforms from protest in crisis to long-term struggle with powerholders to win public majority to oppose official policies and consider positive alternatives. Movement broadens analysis, forms coalitions*

Stage 7: Endgame. *The struggle shifts from opposing official policies to choosing alternatives. More costly for powerholders to continue old policies than adopt new ones. Movement counters powerholders bogus alternatives. Broad-based opposition demands change.*

Stage 8: Success and continuation. *Movement takes on "reform" role to protect and extend successes. The movement attempts to minimize losses due to backlash, and circles back to the sub-goals and issues that emerged in earlier stages.*

I believe that the anti-casino/resiting movements are squarely in Stage 7. Here's what is written about Stage 7:

Stage Seven: Endgame

Stages seven and eight could be called managing success. They are tricky, however, because the game isn't over until it's over. In stage seven, the goals are to recognize the movement's success (not as easy as it sounds!), to empower activists and their organizations to act effectively, to achieve a major objective or demand, and to achieve that demand within the framework of a paradigm shift — a new model or way of thinking about the issue....

Stage seven is a long process, not an event. The struggle shifts in this stage from opposing present policies to creating dialogue about which alternatives to adopt. The movement will have differences within itself about alternatives, and different groups will market different alternatives to the public. The central powerholders will try their last gambits, including study commissions and bogus alternatives, and then be forced to change their policies, have their policies defeated, or lose office....

Each movement needs to develop an endgame which makes sense in terms of its own goals and situation. The fight against nuclear power is an example of change in which there was never a showdown in the United States Congress. Instead, the movement created enough obstacles in the U.S. market to result in a de facto moratorium on new plants, partly by showing them to be unacceptably costly.

In our movement, we are fighting for the endgame, moving from the opposition business of being against the two casinos to the *solutions* business of being either for moving the casinos or getting rid of them entirely.

In our case, two lead organizations represent these two movement goals: the Philadelphia Neighborhood Alliance and Casino-Free Philadelphia are resiting and anti-casino, respectively. Other groups have taken slightly refined, adapted, or anti-*this* casino location positions (strictly NIMBY).

Stage 7 is more than just a discussion of alternatives, though. It is a waged battle with those powerholders who are still holding onto the old policy – i.e. pro-SugarHouse and pro-Foxwoods at their current sites. The loudest politician left is Governor Rendell.

Bill Moyer, the author of MAP, describes this: " Some powerholders change and central, intransigent powerholders become increasingly isolated. Central powerholders try last gambits, then have to change policies, have them defeated by vote or lose office."

Unlike other stages, each movement by them requires an equal *counter-movement* on our part. For example, they try one strategy to get the riparian lands – a last desperate attempt via the city's Commerce Department – and we need to respond. Stage 7 is characterized by *consistent response* to every move the powerholders make. They make a move. We react.

That means at least two things:

The movement is dispersed. Whereas before it was collectively oppositional, now it is split into many different groups each working on the different new and increasingly desperate strategies of the powerholders. This creates an increased sense of isolation among ourselves as the different parts of the movement do *their* part, but it also creates a powerful unison which makes it extremely difficult for the powerholders to gain any traction (hence Rendell's obviously irritated and overstated reaction by calling Council "*gutless*");

The internal movement's differences become exaggerated. Few have missed the PNA's desire to resite while CFP takes a hardline position against casinos. While this was not a huge matter before, now there's a natural shifting as the *endgame* raises the question: what is the *best* way to win? No longer is it enough to be in the big boat together; it is a natural and healthy progression to have our private disagreemnets of strategy now made public.

These are natural phases. Rather than fight them, I suggest we appreciate this moment and declare success that we have come so far.

For more on Bill Moyer's Movement Action Plan, I suggest reading *Doing Democracy* by activist/ scholar Bill Moyer.

Legal Rights

Knowing you legal rights is important to reduce fear, the possibility of danger, and also to know which behaviors are within the law and which are outside of the law.

In this manual, we only *briefly* highlight the likely charges in a blockades scenario (e.g. a site occupation). Before *any* action you should get full briefing from a lawyer or educated activists about the legal implications of the action.

You getting arrested by police, but knowing your rights the whole time.

Casino-Free Philadelphia Previous Actions

In previous Casino-Free Philadelphia actions there have been three charges we thought possible: disorderly conduct (summary offense), resisting arrest (misdemeanor), and trespassing (misdemeanor). We have never been found guilty for breaking *any* law.

Disorderly conduct is a summary offense (like a ticket) and might have a cost to it if found guilty. Resisting arrest is only applicable if someone refuses to go with a police officer or civil affairs officer or disobeys them (not a security guard who in most cases does not have arrest powers). This can include going limp rather than walking with police officers in an arrest scenario. Trespassing is when you are on land which you are not supposed to be on. Generally, but not always, a police officer (or security official) will tell you to leave first.

Only one action of Casino-Free Philadelphia has yet resulted in arrest. In that case for the citizens' document search fourteen people were charged by the Harrisburg police with disorderly conduct. The judge threw out the case and declared all people not guilty (while condemning the PGCB).

Before any action we enlist the help of the National Lawyers Guild to be external observers to our actions. This is to ensure fair treatment by the police and increase our safety.

Secondly, we have lawyers lined up in case we are detained. Pro-bono lawyers specializing in direct actions have agreed to assist us.

Thirdly, we tend to stay in touch with civil affairs, a unit of the police force. Their job is to liaison with direct actionists. We have never had any trouble with them, though we are careful to understand their role is as police officers and therefore have a very different interest than ours in carrying out our action.

And finally, we go through training in the specific action, including advanced scenario planning to map out possible action implications.

CHECKLIST FOR ACTION

What to bring
- food and water, for yourself and to share
- medication in its original pharmacy container
- paper and pens
- emergency phone numbers
- government-issued photo ID

What not to bring
- address book, phone list, planner, or journal
- old ID cards that don't match your current one
- favorite jewelry or expensive electronic devices.

Casino-Free Philadelphia Direct Action Manual

Outline of Legal Steps

STEPS	CHOICES	DESCRIPTION OF WHAT HAPPENS
Warning or Command	– Stay or leave – Don't do or stop doing actions.	Officer may give warning to or leave or command to stop doing something.
Arrest	– Walk with the police – Go limp – Leave the scene	Officer physically grabs you, takes you to police wagon or squad car. May say you are under arrest. Pat search, sometimes handcuffs. Taken to holding area.
Processing and Booking	– Fully cooperate – Decide what, if any, information to give police – Refuse to post bond – Demand no cash bonds or equal bonds for all (bail & jail solidarity)	Police question arrestees concerning information for arrest reports (name/address/occupation/social security number/financial); may try to get additional information for intelligence. Possible photographing/fingerprinting/property and clothes may be taken.
Charging		Prosecutor decides what charges to pursue
First Court Date	– Lawyers or represent yourself – Plea guilty or not guilty – Demand jury trial in future (otherwise likely bench trial)	Appear in court alone, or most likely with other arrestees. Attempt to dispose of case by plea or trial, or continue case for bench or jury trial or plea negotiations later. Prosecutor not always ready for trial.
Trial	– Defense based on noncommission of acts and/or necessity of actions – Small or large resources of time and money	Trials can vary from: a few minute bench trial with or without a lawyer to a full jury trial with expert witnesses lasting a week or more, - or any place in between.
Verdict		Judge or jury decides: - Acquittal (not guilty) - Guilty
Sentencing	– Can testify why actions were justified, necessary, etc., and your background. Sentencing statement is powerful opportunity to bring out political and moral issues. or – Remain silent	Hearing on appropriate sentence

Adapted From: "Organizing for Resistance: Historical and Theological Reflections and Organizing" by the Chicago Religious Task Force on Central America, 1985.

Options for Pleas and Trials

1. **Trial by Judge (Bench Trial):** This is where you would plead not guilty and have your case be heard only by a judge. The judge would presumably listen to the prosecution's witness: (i.e., the police officer) and then your lawyer would cross-examine (ask questions/try to trip up) that witness. Then if you wish or your witnesses could take the stand, tell your side of the story and then be subject to cross-examination. The judge decides if you're innocent or guilty.

2. **Trial by Jury:** This is where you would plead not guilty and have your case be heard by twelve people picked from the community who would listen to the prosecution's and your side of the story. The jury decides your innocence or guilt. In both trial by judge or jury the prosecution has the burden of proving you guilty. In both trial by judge or jury, if you're found guilty the judge decides your sentence.

3. **Pleading Guilty:** This is where you admit to the "crime." You give up your constitutional right to a trial, give up your right to remain silent, give up your right to make the state prove that you are guilty, and give up your right to cross-examine any of the states' witnesses. Presumably, the state gives you a better deal/sentence than if you were found guilty after a trial (either by judge or jury trial).

Potential Sentences

If we are arrested and found guilty, most first-time "offenders" will be offered a period of supervision. Supervision is not a conviction. It is completely erasable from your record (that means you can make the police send back your fingerprints and mug shot) if you complete the supervision successfully and wait two years. Supervision basically means that if you don't get arrested during the period of time (one year, six months, three months, etc) the case is dropped against you. If you do get arrested, for anything except traffic offenses, you could be in violation of your supervision and be resentenced for this charge (plus have your new charge to contend with). As a practical matter few people are violated on supervision, but it is possible.

The range of sentences for misdemeanors include (1) community service, which is not a conviction; you must fulfill a certain number of hours doing community work and must report to a probation officer; (2) conditional discharge, which is a conviction, no reporting; (3) probation – a conviction, and you must report; (4) home confinement – a conviction, stay in your house and be subject to random check-in; (5) jail time – a conviction, stay in jail; (6) pay a fine, a conviction. Any combination of these sentences may be imposed.

From Christian Peacemaker Teams "Legal System Flowchart" as adapted from attorney Melinda Powers September 18, 2003.

Casino-Free Philadelphia Direct Action Manual

Previous Direct Action Campaigns

 **Operation Transparency (October 2006 - January 2007)** – The PA Gaming Control Board (PGCB) refused to make public their documents, such as updated site plans and traffic plans. No meaningful public input could be made without access to such basic documents.

The goal was to get the PGCB to stop violating our right to know and release the hidden documents. If they did not release the documents by our December 1 deadline, we vowed to go to their offices in Harrisburg to carry out a "citizens' document search" to make the documents public ourselves.

We led a two-month campaign with small media-friendly actions, like washing the PGCB's windows to help them become more transparent. After the deadline passed, the documents still had not been released. Fourteen people carried out the document search. All were arrested, only to later be found "Not Guilty" by a judge who scolded the PGCB's behavior. The judge virtually invited us to return to Harrisburg and do it again if the PGCB did not release the documents and become transparent. Public pressure was mounting.

The result: thousands of pages released.

No Way Without Our Say (February - May 2007) – After the Gaming Control Board made its decision to pick SugarHouse and Foxwoods, we vowed to give the public a say in the siting process. We launched No Way Without Our Say – a petition drive to get over 20,000 signatures. That many signatures would force a City Council vote on creating a primary ballot question.

Citizens were asked to support a ballot referendum creating a 1,500-foot buffer between casinos and homes, places of worship, schools, and parks. The goal was to allow Philadelphians a chance to have their voices heard through a legal and open process.

Over 27,000 signatures were gathered in 21 days for the first citizen-initiated referendum in Philadelphia in over thirty years.

The result: once on City Council's desk, they voted unanimously for the referendum (twice!). On May 15th, the voters of Philadelphia would be given the first chance for direct democracy in this casino debacle. But, with a twist...

 **Philly's Ballot Box (May - June 2007)** – Rather than allow the public to have their say, the PA Gaming Control Board, SugarHouse, and Foxwoods sued the City to prevent the vote from going forward.

In a decision reeking of corruption, the PA Supreme Court overruled the city's right and the right of the voters by handing down an injunction that prevented the vote from taking place. A sticker stating, "Removed by Court Order" was placed over the already-printed ballot question on each voting machine. Once again, many politicians, reporters, and pundits declared the anti-casino movement dead.

But we take a bold response to repression. Instead of seeing this as a loss, we saw this as a chance to show the city just how deeply casinos and corruption were intertwined.

In just four weeks, Casino-Free Philadelphia designed and ran Philadelphia's first citizens' election, Philly's Ballot Box. We set up five-foot-tall ballot boxes at polling places in every Councilmanic, State Senate and State Representative district. Over 13,000 people across the city participated in Philly's Ballot Box. 95% said "YES" to the 1,500-foot buffer.

Philly's Ballot Box received local and statewide attention. Even with a competitive Mayoral primary election, we received front-page coverage in the Metro and coverage by TV news channels on election day.

The result: the voters' clear statement in Philly's Ballot Box helped secure City Council's support for the long-term and led to the introduction of the casino buffer question at the state level via House Bill 1477. Yet the greatest result from Philly's Ballot Box was that it renewed people's sense of self-empowerment and creativity in the face of injustice.

Public Filibuster (Fall 2007) – Casino-Free Philadelphia successfully used the "public filibuster" tactic to shut-down the Pennsylvania Gaming Control Board meeting and force them to change policy to allow the public to speak at their "public" hearings.

The public filibuster tactic is an extension of the procedural filibuster. The concept: talk until the meeting is either canceled or time expires. In practice, this action may include members of the public being escorted out of the room, possibly arrested, closing the meeting to the public, or a successful shutting down of the meeting.

Previously, the public was not allowed to testify at the PGCB meetings. At a meeting in fall 2007, several members of Casino-Free Philadelphia stood up, one at a time, during the PGCB board meeting. and started testifying. Each one was gaveled down and told to be quiet by the chairwoman. A recess was immediately called. The three members who spoke – unfortunately all the designated spokespeople – were escorted out of the building and told they would not be allowed to return.

When the board reconvened after recess, the chairwoman warned the group not to continue to interrupt. The remainder of the group immediately stood up and attempted to testify. Another recess was called.

When they reconvened again, the group again attempted to speak up. Finally, she shut down the entire PGCB meeting rather than allow people to speak.

The result: rather than risk another engagement like that, she allowed the public to speak at hearings.

Practice Site Reclamation (December 2007 and ongoing as necessary) – When the state Supreme Court ruled in favor of one of the casinos, effectively mandating that the city of Philadelphia give the casino the zoning permits it needed to begin construction with little

Casino-Free Philadelphia Direct Action Manual

opportunity for further review or delay, we knew it was time for direct action. If we did not up the ante, the casino's story would be that they finally prevailed and their construction was imminent. We needed to show that we were not bowing to the court's decision and would keep pressuring officials who still had options to intervene and stop the construction.

Our campaign exploded into action. In the first five days after the decision we held a large rally, passed out fliers to city workers asking them to slow down the processing of the zoning permits and held a press conference where we pointed out several ways that city and state officials could still intervene to block casino construction.

Most importantly we announced a "practice site occupation" at the end of the week and made it clear that we would follow through on our promise to use civil disobedience at the site of construction if necessary.

When we arrived we found a heavy police presence. We estimated over one-hundred police were on-site and in reserve. Philadelphia's City Police Commissioner, Sylvestor Johnson, personally came to oversee the event. "We're glad you joined," was our attitude, knowing we would also get a chance to show them we were just passionate regular citizens.

A practice site occupation was essentially a direct action training right on or near the site. We did two rounds of role plays for people to practice a scenarios of getting arrested at a future site occupation and blocking a bulldozer. Several members volunteered to play the role of the protestors while others played the police or observed as press.

The result: neither casino has started digging. The political heat keeps getting hotter as politicians are forced to take sides on this increasingly controversial issue resulting in Mayor Nutter taking the side opposing riverfront sites.

 **Operation Hidden Costs (February - April 2008)** – The media still had not covered the underlying costs of casinos. We therefore ran a campaign to talk about the *costs* of casinos.

Gambling brings about severe economic costs, even to those who never set foot in a casino. Those hidden costs to the city include the costs for policing, social service agencies to assist addicts, and prosecuting the rise of crime.

Further, casino slot parlors are being given special treatment by the government, such as exemptions allowing them to serve free drinks all days and all hours. Their introduction will cannibalize millions of dollars from the local economy – another hidden cost.

Governor Rendell never calculated these costs or even explored them. Independent research verifies that his claims of the benefits cannot be trusted. His own financial watchdog agency said the cost of casino-related law enforcement might be as high as $200 million per year, yet he budgeted $0 for such law enforcement.

Our research showed a conservative net loss to the city of at least $52 million per year. To highlight this, we ran a campaign culminating in the first Philadelphia *debate-in* – a lively debate held in the Governor's Philadelphia building.

The result: more substantive news reporting on the costs of casinos than ever before. Further, others echoing us with their own calls for a complete cost/benefit analysis, including City Council and the Mayor.

For More Information

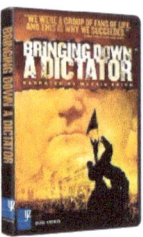

Video: Bringing Down a Dictator

A stunning visual example of how nonviolent direct action works in practice. Using humor and youthful energy, watch how thoughtful citizens in Otpor overthrew one of the most brutal dictators, Slobodan Milosevic in Serbia.

Copies available from: www.aforcemorepowerful.org/order.php

The Politics of Nonviolent Action, by Gene Sharp

The Albert Einstein Institution, 427 Newbury Street, Boston, MA 02115, USA

The authoritative book on the political nature of nonviolence from a highly pragmatic approach. We highly recommend Part One (of Three Parts).

Where Do We Go From Here: Chaos or Community?, by Martin Luther King, Jr.,

New York, Bantam Books 1967

Dr. King's seminal writings on the spiritual discipline of nonviolence and his vision for how nonviolent action could cure the evils of militarism, racism, and poverty.

Also Strength to Love (New York, Harper and Row, 1967) and The Trumpet of Conscience (New York, Harper and Row, 1958).

Website: Training for Change

www.TrainingForChange.org

Training for Change provides training tools, reports, and articles about various aspects of nonviolent action. Its trainers have offered numerous trainings for Casino-Free Philadelphia.

Website: The Ruckus Society

www.Ruckus.org

The Ruckus Society provides hands-on nonviolence training, including blockades and how-to manuals on making various blockades materials.

About the Author

Daniel Hunter is a Training Associate with Training for Change and has led nonviolent direct action, facilitation, and strategy training for a wide range of activists and social change groups. He was Program Director of Training for Change (ending 2005) and works with the Baptist Peace Fellowship's Gavel Fund leading conflict transformation training for social movements across the world.

He has led trainings on five continents for different social justice movements. Those include leading trainings on strategy and conflict transformation with ethnic minorities in Burma/Myanmar, pastors in Sierra Leone, Naga activists fighting for independence in India, environmentalists in Australia, and Indonesian religious leaders. In addition, he has worked with a range of labor, religious, peace & justice and activist organizations in the United States and Canada.

Recently he has offered strategic planning and nonviolent direct action coaching for local and national organizations, including ADAPT, Veterans for Peace, Jobs with Justice, and Ruckus Society. He currently is Strategic Director of Casino-Free Philadelphia, a direct action organization fighting against casino development in Philadelphia.

He was written numerous training manuals nonviolent direct action, including a manual on counter-recruitment and a 630-page manual on third-party nonviolent intervention. That manual, originally co-written by George Lakey for Nonviolent Peaceforce, has set the standard in its field of civilian-based peacekeeping. Civilian interventionists have used it in Zimbabwe, US, Canada, Poland, South Korea, Japan, Ecuador, and elsewhere. Other training manuals he has written include one for grassroots affinity groups on nonviolent intervention and another on nonviolent action for Turn Your Back on Bush, a national peace action.

He is available to local community organizations as a trainer and resource person.

More information, including contact information, available at: www.DanielHunter.org